Unlocking Yo
Family Tree Research Guide

Chapters:

Foreword

Genealogy research is a fascinating and rewarding endeavor. It allows us to uncover the stories of our ancestors, to understand the forces that shaped our families, and to connect with our past in a profound way. But for many people, the idea of starting a genealogy research project can be daunting. Where do you begin? What resources are available? How do you organize and preserve your findings?

The good news is that with a little guidance, anyone can learn the skills necessary to trace their ancestry. And that's exactly what this book provides. "Unlocking Your Family Tree: A Research Guide" is a comprehensive guide that covers all the essential aspects of genealogy research, from organizing your research to advanced techniques like DNA testing and archival research.

Whether you're just starting your family history journey or are a seasoned researcher looking to expand your knowledge, this book has something to offer. Each chapter is filled with practical tips and advice and is accompanied by examples and case studies. Whether you're looking to trace your immigrant ancestors, chart your family tree, or preserve historical materials, you'll find the information you need in these pages.

So, if you're ready to unlock the secrets of your past and build a deeper understanding of your ancestry, this book is for you. It will provide you with the tools and knowledge you need to embark on a journey of discovery and to make meaningful connections with your family's past.

Mark Itdown.

Chapter 1: Introduction to Genealogy

Genealogy, also known as family history research, is the study of one's ancestors and lineage. It is a fascinating and rewarding hobby that allows individuals to learn about their past and connect with their family's heritage. Genealogy research can uncover stories, facts and details about one's ancestors that would otherwise be lost to time.

To begin your genealogy research, it is important to start with yourself and work backwards. Gather as much information as you can about your parents, grandparents, great-grandparents, and so on. This includes their full names, birth dates, marriage dates, and death dates. Any additional information, such as occupation, place of birth, or religious affiliation, can also be helpful.

Once you have a basic understanding of your immediate family, you can start to expand your research. There are many resources available for genealogy research, including online databases, archives, and libraries. Many of these resources offer access to census records, immigration records, birth and death records, and other vital records that can provide valuable information about your ancestors.

Another important aspect of genealogy research is the use of primary and secondary sources. Primary sources, such as birth certificates, marriage licenses, and death certificates, provide first-hand information about an event or person. Secondary sources, such as family histories, genealogy books, and newspaper articles, provide information about an event or person that was recorded by someone who was not present at the time. Understanding the difference between primary and secondary sources and how to effectively use them in your research is crucial.

Organization is key in genealogy research. Keeping track of the information you find, and its source is important. Many genealogy researchers use software or online tools to create family trees and organize their research. It is also helpful to collaborate with other genealogy enthusiasts, either through online forums or local genealogy societies, as you may be able to share information and advice.

Genealogy research can be a time-consuming and sometimes frustrating endeavour, but it can also be incredibly rewarding. Uncovering new information about your ancestors and learning about your family's history can give you a deeper understanding of who you are and where you came from. With the right resources, organization, and determination, you can unlock the secrets of your past and build a rich and meaningful family tree.

Chapter 2: Organizing Research

Organization is key to successful genealogy research. With so many resources available and so much information to collect and sift through, it can be easy to become overwhelmed. However, by developing a system for organizing your research, you can stay on top of the information you've gathered and make it easy to access and use.

One of the first steps in organizing your research is to create a family tree. This is a visual representation of your ancestors and their relationships to one another. There are many software programs and online tools available that make it easy to create and manage a family tree. These tools allow you to enter information about each ancestor, such as names, birth dates, and death dates, and then connect them to other members of the family.

Another important aspect of organization is keeping track of your sources. Whenever you find a piece of information about an ancestor, it's important to record where it came from. This could include a citation for an online database, the title of a book, or the name of an archive. By keeping track of your sources, you'll be able to go back and verify the information if needed, and also make sure that you're not duplicating research.

Another way to organize research is to use a research log. A research log is a record of the research you have done and the sources you have used. This can include the date, the place you researched, what you found and any notes or observations you made. It helps you to keep track of where you have been and where you still need to look. It also helps you to remember what you were looking for and what you found.

Another tip is to use folders, binders, or digital files to separate and organize your research by family line or by location. This will make it easy to find the information you need and keep it separate from other research.

Finally, it's important to take the time to review and analyze the information you've gathered. As you learn more about your ancestors, you may discover new connections or realize that some of the information you have is incorrect. By regularly reviewing your research, you can make sure that your family tree is accurate and up to date.

In summary, organization is key to successful genealogy research. By creating a family tree, keeping track of your sources, using a research log, organizing your research and regularly reviewing the information you've gathered, you'll be able to stay on top of the information you've collected and make the most of your research.

Chapter 3: Online Resources for Genealogy Research

The internet has revolutionized genealogy research by making a wealth of information and resources available to researchers at the click of a button. Online resources include databases, archives, and websites that provide access to a wide range of records, including census records, vital records, immigration records, and more.

One of the most popular online resources for genealogy research is Ancestry.com. This website offers a variety of subscription-based services, including access to census records, vital records, immigration records, and more. Ancestry.com also offers a large collection of digitized books, newspapers, and other publications, as well as the ability to create and share family trees.

Another popular website for genealogy research is FamilySearch.org, which is operated by the Church of Jesus Christ of Latter-day Saints. It offers access to a wide range of records, including census records, vital records, and immigration records, as well as a variety of other resources such as digitized historical books and access to the Family History Library in Salt Lake City, Utah.

Online resources also include a variety of archives and libraries. Many of these institutions have digitized their collections and made them available online, providing researchers with access to a wide range of records and documents. For example, the Library of Congress has a collection of digitized historical newspapers and books available on its website.

Additionally, there are many online forums and social media groups dedicated to genealogy research. These groups provide a platform for researchers to share information, ask questions, and collaborate with others. These groups can also be a great way to connect with others who are researching the same ancestors or regions as you.

It's important to be aware of online resources and how to use them effectively. Some websites may require a subscription or payment to access certain records and some records may only be available at certain libraries or archives. It's also important to be aware of the reliability of the information found on the internet. Before using any information found online, it's important to verify it with a secondary source or by contacting the organization that provided the information.

In summary, online resources are an invaluable tool for genealogy research. They provide access to a wide range of records and documents, as well as the ability to connect with other researchers and share information. By knowing how to effectively use these resources, you can greatly enhance your genealogy research and uncover new information about your ancestors.

Chapter 4: Vital Records for Genealogy Research

Vital records, also known as civil registration records, are official government documents that record significant life events such as births, marriages, and deaths. These records are a valuable resource for genealogy research as they provide detailed information about an ancestor's life, including their full name, birth date, and other key details.

Birth records, also known as birth certificates, are the most basic form of vital record and provide information such as the child's full name, date of birth, place of birth, and the names of the parents. These records can be used to verify an ancestor's birth date and place, as well as to discover the names of their parents and other relatives.

Marriage records, also known as marriage licenses, provide information about the couple's names, the date and place of marriage, and the names of their parents. These records can be used to verify marriage information and to discover the names of the couple's parents, which can be useful in identifying additional ancestors.

Death records, also known as death certificates, provide information about the deceased person's full name, date of death, place of death, and cause of death. These records can be used to verify an ancestor's death date and place, and to learn more about the circumstances surrounding their death.

Vital records are typically maintained by the government and can be obtained from various sources such as the county clerk, state archives, or the national archives. In some cases, the records are available online and can be accessed remotely. Some records may require payment of a fee or proof of relationship to the ancestor in question.

It's important to note that vital records were not always required by government and may not exist for all ancestors, especially those who lived in rural areas or in the early days of the country. Also, some records may have been lost or destroyed due to natural disasters, war or other reasons. However, even if you can't find vital records for an ancestor, other records such as census records or church records, can also provide useful information about their life and family.

In summary, vital records are a valuable resource for genealogy research as they provide detailed information about an ancestor's life. Birth, marriage, and death records can be used to verify key information about an ancestor and to discover new information about their parents, siblings, and other relatives. Obtaining vital records may require some effort, but the information they contain can be invaluable in building a comprehensive family history.

Chapter 5: Tracing Immigrant Ancestors

Tracing the history of immigrant ancestors can be a challenging but rewarding task. Immigrants often leave behind few records in their country of origin, and many records in their new country may be difficult to find or interpret. However, with persistence and a good understanding of the resources available, it is possible to uncover the history of immigrant ancestors and understand their journey to a new country.

One of the key resources for tracing immigrant ancestors is immigration records. These records, also known as passenger lists, provide information about the immigrants' name, age, occupation, and place of origin, as well as the name of the ship they arrived on and the date of their arrival. Immigration records can be found at various archives and libraries, such as the National Archives, or online through websites such as Ancestry.com or FamilySearch.org.

Another important resource for tracing immigrant ancestors is naturalization records. These records document an individual's process of becoming a citizen of their new country and can provide information about an ancestor's name, date of arrival, and place of origin. Naturalization records can be found at various archives and libraries, such as the National Archives, or online through websites such as Ancestry.com or FamilySearch.org.

Census records can also be helpful in tracing immigrant ancestors. The U.S. Federal census has been taken every ten years since 1790, and provides information about an individual's name, age, place of birth, occupation, and other details. Census records can be found at various archives and libraries, such as the National Archives, or online through websites such as Ancestry.com or FamilySearch.org.

Another way to trace immigrant ancestors is to research their country of origin. This can include looking into records such as church records, military records, and land records. These records may be held in archives or libraries in the country of origin, or they may be available online through websites such as FamilySearch.org or through international genealogy societies.

It's important to note that many records of immigrant ancestors may be written in a foreign language and may require some understanding of genealogy research in that language. This can include understanding the handwriting, the naming conventions, and the culture of the time.

In summary, tracing the history of immigrant ancestors can be a challenging but rewarding task. Immigration and naturalization records, census records, and research in the country of origin are all key resources for uncovering the story of immigrant ancestors. With persistence and a good understanding of the resources available, it is possible to uncover the history of immigrant ancestors and understand their journey to a new country.

Chapter 6: Charting Your Family Tree

Creating a family tree is an essential step in genealogy research. A family tree is a visual representation of your ancestors and their relationships to one another. It allows you to see the connections between different branches of your family and can help you to identify potential gaps in your research.

There are many ways to chart your family tree, from simple hand-drawn diagrams to more advanced software programs. The most important thing is to choose a method that works for you and that you will be able to maintain and update easily.

One popular method for charting a family tree is to use genealogy software. These programs, such as Ancestry.com, Family Tree Maker, and Gramps, allow you to enter information about your ancestors and then connect them to other members of the family. They also allow you to add photos, documents, and sources, and to share your family tree with others.

Another way to chart your family tree is to use a family tree template, which can be found online or in genealogy books. These templates provide a basic structure for your family tree, including spaces for names, birth dates, and other key information. They can be filled out by hand or using a computer program.

Another way is to use a pedigree chart. This is a chart that only shows direct ancestors, typically the father and mother of the person at the top of the chart, and is usually limited to several generations. This can be useful to focus on a specific branch of your family tree.

A descendant chart, also known as an Ahnentafel chart, shows the descendants of an individual, starting with the individual and working down to the current generation. This is useful to show the descendants of a specific ancestor, and can be a good way to identify potential gaps in your research.

Regardless of the method you choose, it's important to keep your family tree up-to-date and to include sources for the information you've included. This will make it easier to verify the information and to identify any errors.

In summary, charting your family tree is an essential step in genealogy research. It allows you to see the connections between different branches of your family and can help you to identify potential gaps in your research. There are many ways to chart your family tree, from simple hand-drawn diagrams to more advanced software programs, the most important thing is to choose a method that works for you and that you will be able to maintain and update easily.

Chapter 7: Sharing Your Research

Sharing your research is an important aspect of genealogy. Not only does it allow you to connect with other researchers and family members, but it also helps to preserve your research for future generations. There are many ways to share your research, including creating a family history book or website, collaborating with other researchers, or joining a genealogy society.

One of the most popular ways to share your research is by creating a family history book. This can be a physical book, or an electronic book, that includes information about your ancestors, along with photographs, documents, and other historical artifacts. Creating a family history book allows you to share your research with family members and future generations, and can also serve as a valuable resource for other researchers.

Another way to share your research is by creating a website. A website allows you to share your research with a wider audience, and can include information about your ancestors, photographs, documents, and other historical artifacts. Websites can be created for free using platforms such as WordPress, or by purchasing a domain and hosting.

Collaborating with other researchers is also a great way to share your research. This can include working on a shared family tree, sharing information and resources, or even co-authoring a family history book. Collaboration can help to fill in gaps in your research and can also provide valuable insights and perspectives.

Joining a genealogy society can also be a great way to share your research. Genealogy societies are groups of individuals who are interested in genealogy and family history research. They often provide resources, such as online databases, publications, and events, as well as opportunities to connect with other researchers.

It's also important to be aware of privacy concerns when sharing your research. Personal information, such as dates of birth, death, and marriage, should not be shared without the consent of living individuals. Additionally, it's important to respect the privacy and property rights of others when using and sharing information from sources such as photographs or documents.

In summary, sharing your research is an important aspect of genealogy. It allows you to connect with other researchers and family members, and helps to preserve your research for future generations. There are many ways to share your research, including creating a family history book or website, collaborating with other researchers, or joining a genealogy society. It is important to be aware of privacy concerns and respect the rights of others when sharing your research.

Chapter 8: DNA Testing for Genealogy Research

DNA testing has become an increasingly popular tool for genealogy research in recent years. DNA testing can provide information about an individual's ancestry, ethnicity, and even living relatives. There are several types of DNA tests available, each with its own unique benefits and limitations.

The most common type of DNA test for genealogy research is the autosomal DNA test. This test analyzes a person's autosomal DNA, which is inherited from both parents and can provide information about an individual's ethnicity and ancestry. This test can also identify potential relatives within several generations, including distant cousins.

Another type of DNA test is the Y-DNA test, which analyzes the Y chromosome passed down from father to son. This test can be used to trace the paternal line and can provide information about the origin of a surname.

Mitochondrial DNA (mtDNA) test is another type of DNA test that analyzes the DNA passed down from the mother to both male and female children. This test can be used to trace the maternal line and can provide information about the origin of the mother's line.

It's important to note that DNA testing is not a substitute for traditional genealogy research and should be used in conjunction with other research methods. DNA test results should be viewed as a starting point for further research, and should be verified with traditional genealogical sources such as census records, vital records, and other documents.

Additionally, it's important to be aware of the privacy and security concerns when using DNA testing services. Many companies that offer DNA testing services store the DNA samples and results on their servers and use them for research and data analysis. It's important to understand the terms of service and privacy policy of the company and to ensure that your DNA data is protected and used in accordance with your preferences.

In summary, DNA testing has become an increasingly popular tool for genealogy research. DNA testing can provide information about an individual's ancestry, ethnicity, and even living relatives. However, it's important to note that DNA testing is not a substitute for traditional genealogy research and should be used in conjunction with other research methods. Additionally, it's important to be aware of privacy and security concerns when using DNA testing services.

Chapter 9: Collaboration and Genealogy Societies

Collaboration and genealogy societies are important resources for genealogy research. Collaboration allows researchers to share information, resources, and perspectives, while genealogy societies provide access to resources, expert advice, and a community of like-minded individuals.

Collaborating with other researchers is a great way to share information, resources and expertise. This can include working on a shared family tree, sharing information and resources, or even co-authoring a family history book. Collaboration can help to fill in gaps in your research and can also provide valuable insights and perspectives. Online platforms such as Ancestry.com, FamilySearch.org and MyHeritage.com allow researchers to collaborate and share their research with others.

Genealogy societies are another valuable resource for genealogy research. These are groups of individuals who are interested in genealogy and family history research. They often provide resources, such as online databases, publications, and events, as well as opportunities to connect with other researchers. Genealogy societies can also provide expert advice and guidance on specific research topics.

Joining a genealogy society can also be a wonderful way to share your research with others. Many genealogy societies have online forums, social media groups, or newsletters that allow members to share their research and collaborate with other members. Societies may also organize events such as lectures, workshops, and conferences that provide opportunities for researchers to share their findings and gain new insights.

It is important to be aware that collaboration and genealogy societies can have their own set of rules and protocols. It is important to read and understand these rules before participating in a society or collaboration. It's also important to respect the privacy and property rights of others when sharing information or collaborating.

In summary, collaboration and genealogy societies are important resources for genealogy research. Collaboration allows researchers to share information, resources and perspectives, while genealogy societies provide access to resources, expert advice, and a community of like-minded individuals. Joining a genealogy society can also be a fantastic way to share your research with others, it's important to be aware of the rules and respect the privacy and property rights of others when sharing information or collaborating.

Chapter 10: Archival Research

Archival research is the process of searching for and analyzing historical documents and artifacts. This type of research is essential for genealogy research as it can provide information about an ancestor's life, including their occupation, residence, and family relationships.

When conducting archival research, it's important to start by identifying the types of records that are available for the time period and geographic area of interest. This can include census records, wills, deeds, probate records, church records, military records, and more. These records may be held at various archives and libraries, such as the National Archives, state archives, or local libraries. Many of these records are also available online through websites such as Ancestry.com or FamilySearch.org.

When conducting archival research, it's important to understand the context of the records and the historical events that may have affected them. For example, records may have been lost or destroyed due to natural disasters or war, or they may have been created during a time of political or social upheaval. Understanding the context of the records can help to interpret the information they contain and to identify any potential gaps in the research.

It's also important to be aware of the limitations of archival research. Some records may be difficult to find or interpret, and the information they contain may be incomplete or inaccurate. Additionally, some records may not exist for all ancestors, especially those who lived in rural areas or in the early days of the country.

In summary, archival research is an essential aspect of genealogy research as it can provide valuable information about an ancestor's life. It's important to start by identifying the types of records that are available, and to understand the context of the records and the historical events that may have affected them. Archival research can be challenging, but with persistence and a good understanding of the resources available, it's possible to uncover a wealth of information about your ancestors.

Chapter 11: Oral History

Oral history is the collection and study of historical information passed down through generations by word of mouth. This type of research is important for genealogy research as it can provide valuable information about an ancestor's life, including personal stories, family traditions, and cultural practices.

When conducting oral history research, it's important to start by identifying potential sources of information. This can include family members, community members, and experts on local history. It's also important to be aware that oral history can be influenced by memory and interpretation, so it's important to cross-reference information with other sources.

When conducting oral history research, it's important to use appropriate interviewing techniques. This can include using open-ended questions, allowing the interviewee to tell their story in their own words, and using recording equipment to capture the interview. It's also important to be respectful of the interviewee and to maintain their privacy.

Oral history research can provide valuable information about an ancestor's life, including personal stories, family traditions, and cultural practices. However, it's important to be aware that oral history can be influenced by memory and interpretation, so it's important to cross-reference information with other sources.

In summary, oral history is an important aspect of genealogy research as it can provide valuable information about an ancestor's life, including personal stories, family traditions, and cultural practices. When conducting oral history research, it's important to start by identifying potential sources of information, use appropriate interviewing techniques, and cross-reference information with other sources. Additionally, it's important to respect the privacy of the interviewees and maintain a sense of cultural sensitivity. Oral history research can be a powerful tool for gaining a deeper understanding of your ancestors' lives and the cultural and social context in which they lived.

Chapter 12: Preservation and Conservation

Preservation and conservation are important aspects of genealogy research, as they ensure that historical documents, photographs, and artifacts are preserved for future generations. This includes proper storage, handling, and care of these materials to prevent deterioration and damage.

When preserving and conserving historical materials, it's important to consider the type of material and its condition. This can include using acid-free paper and folders for documents, UV-protective sleeves for photographs, and appropriate storage containers for artifacts. It's also important to keep these materials in a cool, dry place, away from direct sunlight, and to avoid handling them excessively.

Digital preservation is also important, as it ensures that digital documents, photographs, and other materials are accessible in the future. This includes creating backup copies, using appropriate file formats, and using digital preservation software.

It's also important to be aware of copyright laws when preserving and conserving historical materials. This includes obtaining permission from copyright holders before reproducing or sharing materials, and properly citing sources when using historical materials for research or publication.

In summary, preservation and conservation are important aspects of genealogy research, as they ensure that historical documents, photographs, and artifacts are preserved for future generations. This includes proper storage, handling, and care of these materials, and being aware of copyright laws. Digital preservation is also important, as it ensures that digital documents, photographs and other materials are accessible in the future. By preserving and conserving historical materials, genealogists can ensure that these materials are available for future generations to learn from and appreciate.

In conclusion, tracing your ancestry can be a challenging but ultimately rewarding endeavor. "Unlocking Your Family Tree: A Research Guide" has provided you with a comprehensive overview of the various techniques and resources available for genealogy research. We hope that you have found this guide to be helpful and informative in your quest to discover your family history. Remember, genealogy research is an ongoing process, and new information and technology are constantly emerging. We encourage you to continue to learn, explore and discover your family's past and keep your research organized and preserved for future generations. Good luck in your journey!

Made in United States
Troutdale, OR
07/20/2023

11440310R00030